When a Judge Can't Judge
- Part Two
(The Conclusion)

By

Nelson L. Moody, Sr.

ISBN: 1-4033-7894-0 (e-book)
ISBN: 1-4033-7895-9 (Paperback)

Library of Congress Control Number: 2002094661

This book is printed on acid free paper.

Printed in the United States of America
Bloomington, IN

stBooks – rev. 10/07/02

ACKNOWLEDGMENTS

First and foremost I want to thank God for orchestrating my life the way he intended it to be. I thank Jesus Christ for enduring pain, humiliation, mockery, etc. while not saying a word as he was crucified and died for my sins. I thank Moses for obeying God as he freed his people out of slave and bondage. This is who I felt like and now even more as I prepare myself to do what God has ordered in my life, to free men, women, and children. This will enable more men to appreciate this book : When A Judge Can't Judge- Part Two (the conclusion).

To my son, I thank God for letting me be a part of your life. Too many times when a man and a woman end their relationship with each other, the man will (a lot of times) end the relationship with his child/children also. You see I stayed a part of your life after my divorce, besides you are my name sake. I love you.

To The Police Department, I do thank you for doing your job in my case. You guys and gals sometimes don't get the credit you deserve, especially when it comes down to child abuse cases. To Law Enforcement Agencies worldwide keep up the good work especially in cases like mine. To the two officers who took the reports, thanks, I'll meet you one day. To the officers who took the photos, I'll meet you one day also. GOOD JOB AND THANKS.

To doctors who experience cases like mine, I'm glad you investigate closely to see how bruises and marks get on children.

To Mr. Glenn Williams and Mr. J. Edward Whitehead for your financial support in getting "When A Judge Can't Judge- Part Two" (the conclusion) off the ground. A few people talked like they were going to help me. You two men not only talked the talk, you two men walked the walk. Thanks and may you two be forever blessed.

To Educators, don't be afraid to get involved with a child/children who you have knowledge of being victims of child abuse. You could be saving the child/children from future incidents. Protect the child/children, not your degree. Your child/children can be victims one day and their teacher may not want to get involved.

To Social Workers, don't be afraid to take action in a child abuse case over your supervisor's head if he or she don't take the appropriate steps to safe guard the child/children. Don't worry about protecting your title, position, or degree. Protect the child/children. I f that becomes a problem you need to change your profession.

To future attorneys, make sure your client is telling you the truth and can effectively produce facts, proof, evidence, and pertinent information along with creditable witnesses. Don't look at your profession as money, but look at it as you can make a change.

To attorneys, don't fall victim to what my opposing side fell victim of. Make sure that client of yours is telling you the truth. Make sure that same client can produce facts, proof, evidence, pertinent information, and creditable witnesses. Some body out their will do the same thing I did with the court system.

To judges, make sure your attorneys are presenting the best facts, proof, evidence, pertinent information, and creditable witnesses they can present. PEOPLE WHO PRESENT FALSE AND/OR MISLEADING INFORMATION WITH NO KNOWLEDGE OF THE CASE IT SELF DO NOT QUALIFY AS CREDITABLE WITNESSES. People's lives are in front of you. REMEMBER YOUR OATH TO JUDGE CASES FAIRLY AND PARTIALLY BASED ON THE EVIDENCE BEING PRESENTED TO YOU.

DEDICATION

This book is dedicated to God for creating me before I was a thought. For being the creator of every thing. For being there when I wasn't there. For carrying me when I was unable to carry myself (and it was plenty of times I felt this way). Thank you God for patience, endurance, tolerance, discretion, and holding my tongue when I wanted to say things to those who persecuted me, especially the judges and the attorneys.

To Jesus Christ for his much suffering and humiliation. For him not mumbling a word while being persecuted, and for the pain he endured just to save me from and forgive my sins. I have truly learned humility and how to be greatly humble in my situation. To Noah, who kept doing what God told him to do even when every one laughed at him.

To my son for listening to me while talking about different things that has come to past. I do pray that you don't go through the same situation I went through. If you do remember what I told you in your face and in "When A Judge Can't Judge" (my nightmare of the court system in Baltimore, Md.). Just in case you forgot or don't remember I said, "if you find your self in my situation in life, and your mother voice her opinion, be the second person to tell her,"this is how you did my father and I, remember". I'll be the first one to tell her.

TABLE OF CONTENTS

ABOUT THE BOOK

This is the follow up book to "When A Judge Can't Judge "(my nightmare of the court system in Baltimore, Md.). This book still tell how I was treated in the court system in Baltimore, Md. I'm still representing myself in my case. The opposing side still not able to produce any facts, proof, evidence, creditable witnesses, or pertinent information to serve "What's in the child's best interest", according to The Annotated Code of Maryland - Family Law. If nothing was done wrong on July 1, 1996, I would not have taken my case to The Supreme Court Of The United States. All I wanted was justice. "When A Judge Can't Judge (my nightmare of the court system in Baltimore, Md.. bought awareness to some men like me, who is in their child/children's life get treated in the court system, when it comes down to "What's in the best interest of the child?". When A Judge Can't Judge-Part Two (the conclusion) will bring change, reform, and reconstruction of the court system(as it pertains to cases like mine and others with LAW CHANGES). PRAYERFULLY, "WHAT'S IN THE CHILD'S BEST INTEREST WILL BE THE FOCUS.

To my son, always strive to do your best in life and God will do the rest, if you believe. Always be able to JUSTIFY what you're striving for, believing in, and standing up for. Let NO ONE take away from you what you believe in. Remember this, if you don't stand for something, you'll fall for any thing.

Nelson L. Moody, Sr.

In Loving Memory of a little girl I've never met, but she will always be in my heart and memory. We all have to leave this earth one day, but she left with people knowing she was being abused and no one responded quick enough with evidence to show she was being abused. Because of the negligence of the system she died a horrible and terrible way that no one deserve, especially a child. I love you little girl. In Loving Memory also to children who have lost their lives as a result of Department of Social Services, Child Protective Services, and The Court System putting them back into the same hostile environment from which they came from instead of putting them in a safe environment using common sense first, the law second.

PREFACE

No one in The State of Maryland's Judicial System, who was school trained in The Field of Law could JUSTIFY ANYTHING when it came down to "What's in my son's best interest?", but me. They (the judges, attorneys, and master) before me COULD NOT PROVE NOTHING AGAINST ME AS IT PERTAINED TO MY CASE. NO CONCLUSION, DECISION, OR ENDING OF ME COULD BE JUSTIFIED IN ANY WAY, SHAPE, FORM, OR FASHION BY THE COURT SYSTEM OF THE PEOPLE MENTIONED. The mother, R.N., and the school volunteer couldn't PRODUCE ANY FACTS, PROOF, EVIDENCE, PERTINENT INFORMATION, OR CREDITABLE WITNESSES OF WHAT THEY testified to. The mother and the attorneys always made excuses, couldn't produce facts, evidence, or pertinent information of "What's in my son's best interest" on all court dates and no one in the court system picked up on it that should have. They also made PLENTY OF CONTRADICTORY STATEMENTS ,while the attorneys presented perjured testimony and items to court time after time. Still no one pick up on THE MISTAKES OF THE COURT SYSTEM THAT SHOULD HAVE. The mother of all people involved in my case COULDN'T PROVE NOTHING when it came down to "What's in my son's best interest?". That's a shame, help me ladies, gentlemen, and CHILDREN. I was dealing with four "quote un quote" family judges. It was hard believe, fact. It's been said plenty of times that," I, Nelson L. Moody, Sr. was making the judges LOOK INCOMPETENT AT THEIR JOBS when it came down to "What's in the best interest of my son?". I was even complimented by two judges. I know the case better than any one. They couldn't handle my INTELLIGENCE while going through this. It was an open and shut case. A 9 or 10 year old child could have heard my case on July 1, 1996 and gave a better conclusion than the one I got. A 10 To 12 year old child could have judged it better than the judges who were before me. I say,"they were before me because I knew my case better than them". I knew and still know the law as it pertains to my case. To court systems around the world, MEN ARE PARENTS TOO, TO TAKE IT DEEPER AFRICAN-AMERICAN (NEGRO, BLACK MEN),OF WHICH SOCIETY SEEM TO ONLY HIGH LIGHT, SHOWCASE, OR BRING OUT THE NEGATIVE ABOUT US. WAKE UP, WE ARE SOME POSITIVE MEN TOO.

This is a more informative book than "When A Judge Can't Judge (my nightmare of the court system in Baltimore, Md). This is the book that will have people looking at the court system at a different angle. This book will also be the back up of "When A Judge Can't Judge (my nightmare of the court system in Baltimore, Md.), to change the court system when it comes down to "What's in the child's best interest?". It will and can help some one out in a case like mine to beat the odds that are against them. It will also have judges and attorneys (who are like the one's I had),to make sure they have ALL the facts, proof, evidence, pertinent information, and creditable witnesses before they make any decision. This way they don't look incompetent like the one's I was dealing with. The attorneys out their doing their job, according to what's right (by way of common sense),then by the degree of which you have a privilege to practice, I commend you. You are the one's who people can have some respect for and don't mind recommending to a family member or a friend for some thing.

CHAPTER ONE -

GOD (The Alpha & The Omega)

"God works in mysterious ways", my grandmother always said to me when I was a child. God comes when he wants to come, not when you want him to come", she said this also. "He may not come when you want him, but he's on time", she also said. "God knows all and sees all, he sits high and look low, and he won't put nothing on you more than you can bare", she said these sayings also. I remember a lot of what my grandmother told me (the wisdom, advice, and the counsel) has impacted my life in a lot of ways. Yes, my grandmother was a great teacher of life. Grandma used to say a lot of things to me as a child. Some I understood, some I didn't until I was older. Some things she went a little into detail, but never gave you the whole answer. She wanted you to do some of your own thinking. And that she did do. Everything in life happens for a reason, Ecclesiastes 3:1- 8. I love you grandma.

Throughout my case I haven't ask the question to God, "Why me?". I was told, "you don't question God". So as I went through it, the spiritual side of me was showing me a lot of different things and I was the one chosen by God to go through what I went through for the sake of others. This was orchestrated to happen to me before I was a thought. I had no control over it. I was just the one chosen and after a while going through it I knew it was one of my purposes for being in existence. I totally accepted it, not knowing what I was in for, but I trusted God to pull me through from a long dark road to the light. I'm a blessed man by God and I just can't help that.

As I examined my situation and what was happening to me that affect so many men in The United States. I couldn't help but to go back to my son's essay of me to make sure I was still the same person he talked about. Time after time it was confirmed to me over and over again, and it sure feels good to have confirmation in anything that you do. I also get confirmation when I read my Bible or hear a sermon. You see I like to look at spirituality and reality to tie the two together for confirmation. Men, women, and children get confirmation from things you set out to do. You must first be able to recognize your purpose for being here (living). Some people walk around for years (twenty-five or more) and never find or know what their purpose is in life. I'm glad I found my purpose (I've been blessed to have a purpose and a mission in life).

It was orchestrated and ordained for me to deliver men from injustice they received from the court system in a case like mine. Also for women who don't or have never appreciated a man doing his parental responsibilities to his child/children, and thirdly for children to watch how a man, who fathers a child, who earns the title "daddy", so they (the sons) can duplicate the same action when they start having children. As for the girls so they would know what qualities a man should have when he want to take her hand in marriage.

Making sure I was still being and walking in my son's essay steps I still taught, and was able to still lead by example. All of which was a teaching of what I stand for and believe in so that the cycle of fatherlessness will be broken for ever. This can happen IF EVERY MAN WITH CHILDREN PLAY A GOOD STRONG ROLE IN THE LIFE OF THEIR CHILD/CHILDREN. Especially if he and the mother are no longer together. Let's face it people break up and married people divorce (look at me). It shouldn't stop the relationship you as a man have with your children. This is special if the father and the mother are not living together in the same household. No court system should have to intervene with nothing involving you and your child/children. Unfortunately it happens and unless things (a lot) are recognized by the court system men will always be at a disadvantage (the good ones). Because you wear a skirt and bare a child don't make you no mommy. This is the opposite of any man can be a father, but it takes someone special to be a daddy. You the reader, examine yourself just to see where you fit in.

As I look back on my life and my court case, my faith in God has been there and I refuse to let anyone or anything change, alter, or try to persuade me into believing that God don't exist. It's been said, "God will not put anything on you that you can't bare". I believe that, because he brought me a mighty long way. It's been said," "God will never leave you nor forsake you". He never left me . He also said, "I will make your enemies your foot stool", he did (and anything that looks like an enemy). God also said, "no weapon formed against me shall prosper". I believe it. He said, "vengeance is mine". I believe that. God also said, "Nelson L. Moody, Sr., my son, I'll open doors for you no man can close". I believe it and it's happening now. I claimed the victory and spoke it from my mouth. God manifested it.

God has truly shown me that he is real as real can get. He also has shown me what faith (the size of a mustard seed) can do if you believe in him, his son Jesus Christ, and The Holy Spirit. Hebrews ,chapter 11.God has worked on me and through me to show me that with GOD ALL THINGS ARE POSSIBLE. I had EVERYTHING AGAINST ME as I represented myself from The Circuit Court of Maryland in Baltimore, Md. To The Supreme Court of The United States. I have succeeded against all the odds, because God had and still has his hand on me. God carried me, pushed me, and elevated my knowledge that enable me to be taken places I've never been before and opened plenty of doors THAT NO MAN CAN CLOSE. All of this because of my faith in God. No one will ever be able to change my faith in God (spouse, mother, brother, children, etc.).

CHAPTER TWO -

NOVEMBER 1999

As I await my court date in November 1999, the visitation of my son was getting a little better now . I'm glad, but will not think that it won't go back to the way it was.

On August 25, 1999 I received a letter from knucklehead trainee #1 addressed to the judge I saw in August 1999, of whom I'll see on November 17, 1999. It was basically an order. An order that says, "I'm hereby found to be in contempt of court for failing to pay child support", as ordered by the first judge in December 1996 that's in my divorce decree dated January 6, 1997. They also wanted the judge to order me to pay $4,138.80 as of the date of the hearing (November 17, 1999. They wanted the judge to order me to pay $2,000.00 toward arrears by November 17,1999. They also wanted me to start immediately making payments at the rate of $ 92.80 per month via a lien on my wages. Then they had the nerve to remind me of my court date. How could I not remember . I offered my son being on my health insurance. You should have seen knucklehead trainee #2's look when I offered that. You, the reader should be able to see what their focus(money) vs. mine (what's best for my son). Watch who have their stuff together and see who look incompetent Their wage lien order was this: This matter having come before this court for hearing come before this court for hearing on August 13,1999, and the court having determined that (me) Nelson L. Moody, Sr. , the obligor has accumulated support payment of arrears amounting to more than thirty days of support. With this they wanted the court to hereby ADJUDGED, ORDERED AND DECREED : 1. That the child support payments of $92.80 per month, plus payments towards the arrearage in the amount of $100.00 per month, be paid to the obligee, (my son's mother). 2. That a lien issue in the amount of $ 192.80 per month, against the earnings and / or other form of periodic payments due to the obligor, Nelson L Moody, Sr., from (my job), the existing employer of the obligor, and any future employer upon whom a copy of this ORDER may be served ,be and they are hereby directed and ordered to deduct the aforesaid sum from the earnings and/or other form of periodic payment due or to be due the Plaintiff, and remit same to (my son's mother/with her address). (or any other address directed by my son's mother). 4. That the employer may deduct and retain from the obligor's earnings an additional $ 2.00 for each deduction made under this order. 5. That the net amount withheld shall be sent promptly to the obligee at the address specified above. 6. That the employer shall be subject to civil penalties for the willful violation of this order.

They also sent this information to my job. I'm glad that it's good attorneys out there, and not like the one's I 'm dealing with. I can't wait until the two I''m dealing with get put under the microscope and be on trial. The difference between me and them is, when they go on trial everything will be justified. With me they couldn't justify nothing they did and still doing.

While still handling my business with my case, I did file a Petition To Modify Custody. It was played with and denied like everything else. In my Petition To Modify Custody I was able to produce facts, proof, evidence, and pertinent information(as always) to justify what I was doing. While this was going on knucklehead trainee # 1 & 2 tried to get the judge to dismiss my petition . I did laugh because by now I'm a SERIOUS THREAT to them. That's a shame, because they're the one's with the law degree. Not me.

On September 23, 1999 a letter in response to my Petition To Modify Custody was mailed out by knucklehead trainee #1 that read : Now comes the Defendant (son's mother) by Top Attorney and in answer to the Motion To Modify Custody, filed by Plaintiff, and states: 1 & 2 of how she (son's mother) admits to the allegations of paragraph 1 & 2 in part. 3. That she denies the allegations contained in paragraph 3 and further states that the incident refereed to occurred in October of 1996 as evidenced by the attachments to Mr. Moody's pleadings, which was prior to the previous hearing and was raised by Mr. Moody at the time of that hearing. Therefore, there is no change in circumstances since the last order (you will see how the judges in the year 2000 skate and dance around this same issue of circumstances. Whether it happen two days before or two days after the last order. The fact is it happened. Wake up judges and attorneys).They wanted me to pay their client's attorney fees and have my Motion To Modify Custody to be denied.

Anyway I wrote a letter to the Clerk of The Court on September 29, 1999 that went like this:

Dear Mr. Clerk

The following definitions are outlined in the Annotated Code of Maryland, as it pertains to my case. 1. What shall be deemed perjury (with supporting cases) 2.Indictment (along with supporting cases) 3.Contradictory statements (along with supporting cases) A. What shall be deemed perjury (along with supporting cases) B. Indictment (along with supporting cases) C. Contradictory statements (along with supporting cases) D. Subornation of perjury (along with supporting cases) E. Penalty (along with supporting cases). Knucklehead trainee #1 and knucklehead trainee #2 are both guilty of this because they knew from July 1, 1996 when there was nothing to prove what was said about me. The parent volunteer and the R.N. are also guilty of this when they couldn't produce nothing to support what they said about me.

With all this in mind, my Petition To Modify Custody should be granted to the fullest extent. Based on "What's in the child's best interest?". Also my son's mother finally admitting to the allegations, my Petition should definitely be granted.

1. My pleading to modify custody is not frivolous as the top attorney say. If his client had facts, proof, and evidence on July 1, 1996 to show "What's best for the child (my son),we would not be going through this because of his incompetence.

2. The attorneys need to stop concealing "What's in the child's best interest?", according to The Annotated Code of Maryland.

3. October 3, 1996 has presented a change in circumstances since the wrong conclusion of me by the Master(the police department has this proof, a report the mother made).

4. My pleading is as genuine as genuine can be and it speaks the truth about "What's in the child's best interest?".

5. His client (son's mother) do not show or set a good example for the child, by making allegations, perjuring herself by making contradictory statements, then admits to the allegations three years later.

6. The allegations of me were false from the beginning that I talked about in my Brief and Record Extract, and both of my Petitions(The Court of Appeals of Maryland and The Supreme Court of The United States).

7. My son's mother's actions before July 1,1996, after, and to this date have been detrimental to the child's life completely(as in a court case).

WHEREFORE, By the plaintiff, Nelson L. Moody, Sr. request:

A. Plaintiff's Motion to Modify Custody should not be denied.

B. If the case was judged properly by law, according to The Annotated Code of Maryland there would be no need for a Modification of Custody.

C. The Plaintiff, Mr. Nelson L. Moody, Sr. should be compensated enormously for the damages of character, mental injury, libel and slander, etc.

    D. The child need to be compensated also.

    E. Penalties need to be imposed.

    F. The defendant should be ordered to pay reasonable attorney fees to plaintiff (since I'm pro-se) and for such other and further relief as the nature of my cause may require.

    cc. Top Attorney
    cc. Administrative Judge
    cc. Chief Judge of Maryland
    cc. Chief Justice of The Supreme Court
    cc. Ms. Attorney General
    cc. Mr. Bar Counsel
    cc. The Media

                Sincerely,
          Mr. Nelson L. Moody, Sr.

From this letter I got a response from the court by way of The Family Division Coordinator letting me know that my letter written on September 29,1999 has been forwarded to a judge that will be in front of me on January 3,2000 for a scheduling conference. All the judges are from The Family Division. I find that hard to believe, that they are part of The Family Division. Where is the focus put on in my case? Drain Nelson L. Moody, Sr. financially or just drain him. I could not see where the judges or the attorneys (knucklehead trainees #1 & #2) are focused on "what's best for the child". Their day will come and I want to see how they act and their spouses respond to them after they get on the hot seat.

While still handling my business with the court system, I still wondered why they (the judges and attorneys) just couldn't admit that they could not JUSTIFY NOTHING they did or have been doing from the beginning of my case. Maybe they are giving me such a hard time because I'm representing myself with everything being presented to them is on accordance with The Annotated Code of Maryland. Just for thought , people have said, "I'm making them look INCOMPETENT at their jobs as judges and attorneys. I do thank God above for my common sense. I also thank God for how he sits high and look low. I know I'm in God's favor. I wrote this letter to the judge who was before me in August 1999 :

Dear Judge

I started the letter off with some information from The Annotated Code of Maryland- Family Law. With this in mind, it is frustrated to me for the court system to put me through what I'm going through. It's also a shame of how you can be so aggressive to enforce what the top attorney has requested, but don't give an answer or reply to my petition to modify custody (because I have shown that a change of custody is/ was needed) and my letter for you not to grant The Motion To Quash Subpoenas for top attorney, other attorney, and my son's mother. Their subpoenas are relevant to this case. Then you threaten to have me incarcerated.

This case would not have went this far if the Master judged the case by law, by the book (according to The Annotated Code of Maryland) to serve "what's in the child's best interest?''. The Master made a WRONG conclusion of me with no facts, proof, evidence, or pertinent information that would justify her conclusion of me. Then the judge behind her followed her wrong conclusion, and now you're doing it.

It seems like none of the judges (including yourself) are putting any focus on "what's best for the child?'', since July 1, 1996. It's also in :

1. Brief and Record Extract, Court of Appeals of Maryland : September Term 1997 # 479.

2. Petition For Writ of Certiorari, Court of Appeals of Maryland : September Term 1998 # 72.

3. Petition For Writ of Certiorari, The Supreme Court of The United States : October Term 1998 # 98-6124.

To top it all off, my son's mother admits to the allegations and I also showed a change in custody was and is needed since October 3, 1996, when the child (my son) was assaulted by son's mother's husband (then boyfriend) (as in a case from The Annotated Code of Maryland).

Two police officers from the police department even wrote reports that son's mother made. The school police and vice- principal of the middle school my son attended have knowledge of this also. A social worker from Child Protective Services did a complete investigation on October 4, 1996 in my house, indicated it child abuse, but did nothing by law to take the matter to court and remove the child from the house as in The Annotated Code of Maryland : para. 5-907- Actions by local departments and State's Attorney's office. The attorney KNEW OF THIS ALSO.

I've also talked with the attorney on September 20, October 4, and also on October 20, 1999 in reference to my son not being sent to my house when he is suppose to be sent. The last time my son stayed at my house was on August 14, 1999.

No one is putting focus on the child's best interest, but me. Everything is not being taken into consideration as in (a court case in The Annotated Code of Maryland). With the question being, "What's in the child's best interest?". No one is focusing on this, but me. Where are the morals, ethics, values, and standards in this case focused on?. The child's best interest or let's drain Mr. Moody (money). All of this is the result of the Master's WRONG CONCLUSION of me with nothing to prove what was said about me or her conclusion of me. To this day she could not JUSTIFY why she made and how did she come to a conclusion of me with NOTHING TO PROVE WHAT SHE DID.

In closing, one day real soon a lot of people will be saying, "that man had a BIG PROBLEM and no one took the time to investigate it that SHOULD HAVE.

    cc. Top Attorney
    cc. Family Division Coordinator
    cc. Judge for January 3, 2000

cc. Administrative Judge

cc. Chief Judge of Maryland

cc. Chief Justice of The Supreme Court of The United States

cc. The Attorney General of The United States

cc. A Father's Group

cc. The Media

While waiting for my November 17, 1999 court date my son still wasn't being sent to me like he was suppose to be sent. His mother gave an excuse, left the house prior to being sent or just didn't get sent at all. It's all good.

I finally got to court on November 17, 1999, presented what I needed to present and I was still looking good. Knucklehead trainee #2 told the judge, "I have not paid knucklehead $ 2,000.00 as of yet". This was true. The judge asked me, "Why haven't I paid yet?". I showed receipts of the money I paid to knucklehead. He then said, "you know I can have you incarcerated for this".I told him, "I know that, but by law you can't drain me of money and I end up with no place for my son. You do what you got to do". Knucklehead trainee # 2 whisper to knucklehead then told the judge, "It's not her intent to see me incarcerated, she just want the child support".

The judge then mentioned to me to catch up. I said, "okay I'll do that"(in a no caring voice). That's what this whole thing was all about, money instead of "What's best for the child?".

14

CHAPTER THREE -

JANUARY 2000

As the new year rolled in I was ready for my January 3, 2000 court date and also the perjury, mistakes, negligence, etc. from knucklehead trainee's # 1 & 2. Even from knucklehead. I was also looking for the, "who do you think you are coming into my courtroom, knowing the law better than me attitude" from the judges. Well brace yourself because I got both as I anticipated. Two for two. What a score.

It started off with me getting to the courtroom before the opposing side. Once knucklehead trainee #1 came in the courtroom. He had the nerve to ask me, "have I seen his client?" (maybe he thought it was my day to baby sit her, it wasn't).My answer to that question was no. He went into the judges chambers for about six to eight minutes. About ten minutes later the judge called us into the judges chambers. We made each other aware of what was going on, and that I was here to get custody of my son modified and changed to serve "what's in my son's best interest?". The judge did some talking while we listen, but kept making eye to eye contact with knucklehead trainee #2.

While going back and forth with the judge I asked the question, "why when you talk, you tend to look at the attorney and ask him questions about my case pertaining to me, but don't make too much eye contact with me while directing something to me?". I was told, "he's an attorney and knows how the system works". I told her, "I know the laws that surround my case better than him".She didn't like that comment. I offered to show her some of my case and my work I've done on my own. She, like the rest of the judges before her couldn't accept the fact I'm a intelligent man walking in this courtroom with no law degree. Once again she looked incompetent at her profession as a judge (attorney).

If she read the history of my case and can understand what she read. It would have told her a lot about my character, assertiveness, determination, credibility, intelligence, courage, etc. I don't know. Can you, the reader help me out(I have not forgot about you in this book, I want you to still help me out). Since the people who should have helped me, didn't and to think my fatherhood/parenthood was being tested, tried, and played with again. There's not a judge in the court system qualified, certified, or bonafide to do this . ONLY GOD CAN DO THIS.

Knucklehead trainee #2 searched for it also. Guess what I did? I pulled it out without searching for it. They looked at each other after I showed it to them. Guess how they looked? They LOOK REAL STUPID. Remember I'm the one with no law degree, but the one with all the answers. I was truly enjoying this making them look incompetent (with law degrees) at their jobs.

The judge and I went back and forth with words for about two minutes until I was told by her, "this whole thing could end here if I wanted it to end". I quickly shut my mouth and started to bite my tongue for the moment. It was then told to knucklehead trainee #2 , "that I do have a right to have my petition heard". His face dropped hard. A new court date was being arranged and I was writing it down on my paper work also. I got up and told the judge, "have a good day".

I even had photos of the injuries my son sustained when he was assaulted by his mother's husband (boyfriend then). The judge did not want to see them. We soon go out of the chambers. I laughed while smiling at knucklehead trainee #2. I told him, "you have a young daughter. What if your wife take you through the same thing you and knucklehead trainee # 1 is taking me through". He could not give an answer , just a dumb founded look. As knucklehead was turning the corner knucklehead trainee #2 was letting her know that I got my court date. Just before she came around the corner I told knucklehead trainee #2, "I'm going to damage your career". He said to me, "I said that once before". I told him, "believe it, wait and see". I took one last look at the two of them while smiling. My next court date was set for March 29, 2000 @ 9:30a.m.

My son was never sent to my house on January 1, 5, or 7, 2000. Since I was due back in court on March 29, 2000 I decided to let the next judge know just how serious I am about this matter and only hope that they (judges) really look at and examine my case carefully. I would not have came this far if I didn't think nothing was done wrong.

I did my Petition For Contempt (denial of visitation) on January 12, 2000. In my petition I mentioned my son is not being sent to me like he is supposed to be sent. Excuses given for not being sent were: no transportation, or spouse not at the house. Most recent January 1, 2000, January 5, 2000, and January 7, 2000. The last visit with my son was on December 18,1999. My son's mother is now in contempt for failing to obey the order. A part talked about do I want her to get jail time to enforce it's order. I wrote what ever deem necessary. These were my reasons for requesting the court to issue a Show Cause Order and find my son's mother in contempt, enforce visitation, and order any appropriate relief relating to visitation with my son. Too and including modifying and changing custody of the child "to serve what's best for the child", based on facts, proof, evidence, creditable witnesses, pertinent information, and The Annotated Code of Maryland.

On this same day (January 12, 2000), I sent my Interrogatories to support my Petition to Modify/Change custody to the courthouse, knucklehead trainee #2 and knucklehead. This is how the Interrogatories went.

To: My son's mother, Defendant
From : Nelson L. Moody, Sr.
You are hereby requested to answer the following Interrogatories.
   (A) These Interrogatories are propounded pursuant to The Maryland Rules which require that they be answered separately and fully in writing, under oath, within thirty (30) days after service or such shorter time as provided by court order.

(B) Knowledge or information of a party shall include that of the party's employees, agents, representatives and, unless privileged, attorneys. Where an answer is made by a corporate defendant, state the name, address and title of the person supplying the information and making the affidavit, and the source of his information.

(C) The pronoun you or yourself refers to the party to which these Interrogatories are directed.

(D) Where the singular is used with reference to any person, document or item, it shall include the plural, if in fact, there are more than one.

(E) These Interrogatories are continuing in character, so as to require you to file supplementary answers if you obtain further or different information before trial.

(F) Where the name or identity of a person is requested, please state full name, home address and business address, if known.

(G) Unless otherwise indicated, these Interrogatories refer to the time, place, and circumstances of the occurrence mentioned or complained of in the pleadings.

INTERROGATORY NUMBER 1 : List names of creditable witnesses who will be testifying on your behalf.

INTERROGATORY NUMBER 2 : List the occupations of the names of the creditable witnesses who will be testifying on your behalf.

INTERROGATORY NUMBER 3 : List names of creditable witnesses who can say the child is sent to father (Nelson L. Moody, Sr.) at times and days that are specified in court order.

INTERROGATORY NUMBER 4 : List name (s) of any and all members of clergy who has knowledge of the way the child should be sent to father (Nelson L. Moody, Sr.).

INTERROGATORY NUMBER 5 : List of excuses used for not sending the child to the father (Nelson L. Moody, Sr.).

INTERROGATORY NUMBER 6 : List excuses why child was not sent to father (Nelson L. Moody, Sr.) on January 1,2000 at 7:00p.m., January 5, 2000 at 6:30p.m., and January 7, 2000 at 6:30p.m.

INTERROGATORY NUMBER 7 : List reasons, if any, why child has been mentally scarred while in his mother's dwelling.

INTERROGATORY NUMBER 8 : List reasons, if any, why the child has been emotionally scarred while in his mother's dwelling.

INTERROGATORY NUMBER 9 : List reasons, if any, why the child has went through psychological scarring while in his mother's dwelling.

INTERROGATORY NUMBER 10: List reasons as to why you was arrested on October 3, 1996.

INTERROGATORY NUMBER 11 : List reasons as to why you took child to the police department on October 5, 1996.

INTERROGATORY NUMBER 12 : List reasons as to why you went to Eastside Courthouse on November 4, 1996.

INTERROGATORY NUMBER 13 : List the testimony that you gave to the court to have your case nolle prosequi on November 4, 1996.

INTERROGATORY NUMBER 14 : Reflecting back to October 3, 1996, putting yourself in the child's shoes, mind, and body. Do you think that a change of circumstances was needed for the sake of the child?, which would affect the child for the rest of his life.

INTERROGATORY NUMBER 15 : State the reasons as to why you think a change in custody should not happen. Based on everything that has been presented to the court system to show "what's in the child's best interest?". With all the facts, proof, evidence, pertinent information, and highly creditable witnesses. All of which is found in Brief and Record Extract, Court of Special Appeals of Maryland (September Term 1997 # 479), Petition For Writ of Certiorari, Court of Appeals of Maryland (September Term 1998 # 72), and Petition For Writ of Certiorari, The Supreme Court of The United States (October Term 1998 # 98-6124).

The following definitions are outlined in The Annotated Code of Maryland, as it pertains to my case.

A. What shall be deemed perjury (with supporting cases from The Annotated Code of Maryland).

B. Indictment (with supporting cases from The Annotated Code of Maryland).

C. Contradictory statements (with supporting cases from The Annotated Code of Maryland).

D. Subornation of Perjury (with supporting cases from The Annotated Code of Maryland).

E. Penalty (with supporting cases from The Annotated Code of Maryland).

As I got back to my house later that afternoon (January 12), I had mail from knucklehead trainee #1. I opened it to read it. I was surprised that they had the guts to respond to my Petition to Modify Custody. This response came from my letter dated September 29, 1999 along with my Petition to Modify Custody. That's more than (90) ninety days. I never had a problem making any deadlines and time frames, they did. It basically went like this.

Now comes the defendant, son's mother by her attorneys moves to dismiss The Petition/ Motion to Modify Custody filed by the Plaintiff Nelson L. Moody, Sr. and in support there of states as follows :

1. That the only grounds alleged by the Plaintiff for a modification of the previous order of this court is contained in paragraph three of The Petition/Motion, where in he states: circumstances have changed and the order is no longer in the best interest of the child

because the child was assaulted by his mother's husband (then boyfriend) see attached papers (a child assaulted by an adult changes custody to protect the child from future incidents).First it's a COMMON SENSE THING, Secondly, IT'S THE LAW.

2. That the attached papers to which the Plaintiff refers relate to an alleged incident which happened on October 3, 1996. There is nothing alleged about the incident which took place on October 3, 1996. It happened and paperwork show the evidence.

3. That at the hearing for divorce which was held on December 4, 1996, the Plaintiff contested custody and presented evidence concerning the alleged incident of October 3, 1996.

The police department have the report my son's mother made to them which makes the incident not only fact, but true and not alleged. WHAT ARE THE ATTORNEYS TRYING TO HIDE? THE TRUTH WHILE PROTECTING THEIR CAREERS RATHER THAN THE CHILD.

4. That I then appealed the court's order to The Court of Special Appeals of Maryland, The Court of Appeals of Maryland, and The Supreme Court of The United States ; but was unsuccessful at each level. The truth is no one want to investigate the case, judge it by law, by the book to determine "what's in the child's best interest". It seems no one want to over turn the Master's WRONG CONCLUSION OF ME.

5. That I am attempting to raise the same issues which have already been decided, and is presenting no new evidence.

6. That my Petition/Motion to Modify Custody should therefore be dismissed.

WHEREFORE, the Defendant requests :

A. That the Plaintiff's Petition/Motion to Modify Custody be dismissed..

B. That the Plaintiff be ordered to pay the Defendant's attorney fees and the cost of these proceedings.

C. That son's mother be granted such other and further relief as the nature of her cause requires.

By now I'm more of the threat to these two knucklehead attorneys than ever before or what. They are running with their law degrees to hide things. I'm just walking through with my high school diploma and PLENTY OF COMMON SENSE.

Also on January 11, 2000 some one else tried to get information about my case that seem to be from another state. The first time was November 22, 1999. I feel good knowing someone in the United States read something I've sent and came to a conclusion that Mr. Nelson L Moody, Sr. is having a big problem in the court system in Baltimore, Md.

What ever they (attorneys or the court) ask for, I've always presented more than enough information. I'm bad as I want to be. I just know I've got to be their worst nightmare. A man with no law degree making them look stupid and incompetent at their jobs. Could you imagine if I had a law degree?. I'd be SERIOUSLY DANGEROUS. I was already DANGEROUS. Those attorneys and judges should be glad and lucky I'm not licensed to practice law. They should have smoked me long, long, long, time ago. They really should have asked somebody about my fatherhood/parenthood. They choose not to. I turned out to be the most valuable player.

My son wasn't sent to me on Sat. January 15, 2000, Weds. January 19, 2000, or Fri. January 21, 2000. He never came on Weds. January 26, 2000, but did come on Sat. January 29, 2000. It's still all good anyway. I wanted to make sure the court system, the judges, and the attorneys were well aware that I was treated wrong in my court case since July 1, 1996. I wrote another letter to the court that went like this. Written on January 20, 2000

Dear Clerk :

Please accept my Petition/ Motion to Modify Custody in the captioned matter. To and include changing custody. Thank you for your kind cooperation in this matter.

PETITION/MOTION TO MODIFY CUSTODY

Now comes the time when the Plaintiff, Nelson L. Moody, Sr., request that Petition/Motion to Modify Custody, filed by Plaintiff be granted to the fullest extent . In support there of states as follows :

1.   The facts are there to have shown a change in circumstances occurred when the child was assaulted by his mother's husband, who then reported the incident to the police department along with photos (as in a case from The Annotated Code of Maryland).

2.   The incident which happened on October 3, 1996 is not alleged as the attorneys say. It's the truth and it happened.

3.   The attorneys argue that the incident occurred before a order and that no change of circumstances occurred. If a court paper takes precedent over the fact that a child was assaulted and the mother made the report to the authorities, then something is wrong with the judicial system (as it pertains to my case).

4.   The priorities are not where they should be, and no one is focusing on "what's in the child's best interest", except me Nelson L. Moody, Sr.

5.   The attorneys need to stop concealing "what's in the child's best interest" for they have not been able to prove nothing according to The Annotated Code of Maryland.

6. The Plaintiff, Nelson L. Moody, Sr. was and still is able to produce much more facts, proof, evidence, creditable witnesses, and pertinent information in support of this petition as it is outlined in The Annotated Code of Maryland- Family Law.

7. That no one has taken into consideration the child's wishes, anything he said, or anything that he offered to the court (as in a case in The Annotated Code of Maryland).

8. That the child's rights were violated according to The Constitution of The United States, Article 1 (as it pertains to my case).

9. That no one has focused on everything surrounding the custody issue of the child (as in a case in The Annotated Code of Maryland).

10. That a change in custody (as in a case in The Annotated Code of Maryland).

11. That the child don't get sent to Plaintiff's house like he is suppose to.

12. That the child can give his own testimony again as to what goes on. He is also expected to be in court on March 29, 2000 at 9:30a.m. as ordered by judge seen January 3, 2000 as one of the Plaintiff's witnesses for a trial on the merits.

Nelson L. Moody, Sr.

WHEREFORE, the Plaintiff requests:

A. That the Petition/Motion to Modify Custody be granted and not dismissed.

B. That the Defendant and the attorneys be ordered to pay the Plaintiff's attorney fees and the cost of these proceedings. The Plaintiff is pro-se.

C. That the Plaintiff be granted such other relief and further relief of his cause requires.

D. That the attorneys and son's mother produce and tell the truth of "what's best for the child". Taken everything offered to the court into consideration.

c. c. Top Attorney
c. c. Son's mother

Very truly yours,

Mr. Nelson L. Moody, Sr.
Pro-se

CHAPTER FOUR -

POUND FOR POUND

The month of February 2000 came on in and I was still just as good as I was in the previous months. I was just getting better(like wine and cheese) and still the best is yet to come. The judges couldn't take it, this I know. It was like one judge was saying to the next one, "alert, alert be on the lookout for Nelson L. Moody, Sr. Who is coming your way with his smart ass self. He has no law degree, but his paper work is on the money. Stop everything he's trying to do".

My son didn't show up at my house on Weds. February 2, 2002 like he was supposed to.

He didn't come to my house on Fri. February 4, 2000, he ended up coming on Sat. February 5, 2000.

He was a no show on February 9, 2000. It's all good. On February 11, 2000 I received a letter from knucklehead trainee # 1. It was the response to Motion to Modify Custody dated January 20, 2000 found in chapter three.

1. The defendant denies the allegations contained in paragraph #1.

2. The defendant denies the allegations contained in paragraph #2

3. The defendant cannot admit nor deny the allegations contained in paragraph #3 as there is no factual assertion.

4. The defendant cannot admit nor deny the allegations contained in paragraph #4 as there is no factual assertion.

5. The defendant cannot admit nor deny the allegations contained in paragraph #5 as there is no factual assertion.

6. The defendant cannot admit nor deny the allegations contained in paragraph #6 as there is no factual assertion.

7. The defendant cannot admit nor deny the allegations contained in paragraph #7 as there is no factual assertion.

8. The defendant cannot admit nor deny the allegations contained in paragraph #8 as there is no factual assertion.

9. The defendant cannot admit nor deny the allegations contained in paragraph #9 as there is no factual assertion.

10. The defendant cannot admit nor deny the allegations contained in paragraph #10 as there is no factual assertion.

11. The defendant denies the allegations contained in paragraph 11.

12. The defendant cannot admit nor deny the allegations contained in paragraph #12 as there is no factual assertion.

WHEREFORE, the Defendant prays:

A. That the Plaintiff's motion be denied.

B. That the Plaintiff be ordered to pay reasonable attorney fees and costs of these proceedings.

C. For such other and further relief as the nature of her cause may require.

This is one of the first times my son's mother signed her real name on a court document since she remarried July 1998. The attorneys know of all this information. She kept using my last name. A no no. I 've had problems with this in my credit report where it was indicated that I lived in the 1300 block Gorsuch Ave. (this is the house she and her husband lived in when my son was assaulted by husband on October 3, 1996). Why would the three of us be living in the same house. She still use my last name in the phone book in Baltimore, Md. And in other places. I caught a back lash a few times with things left behind that we created together.

As you can see what their excuses were. They used the same one just about all the time. I think knucklehead trainees #1 & 2 were sleeping in law school. They should have had detention and plenty of coach classes. They didn't have no idea they would ever come across my path while in law school one day.

If one thing that these two attorneys have learned about me is that man, Nelson L.. Moody, Sr. is intelligent and he's no dummy. They know this very well. That's why in "When A Judge Can't Judge (my nightmare of the court system in Baltimore, Md.) Chapter thirteen- Intelligence vs. Trainees (Nelson L. Moody, Sr. vs. them). This is where they get their names from (knucklehead trainee #1 & 2). So BEWARE attorneys out there like these two. There are more people out there like me that will challenge attorneys and the court system. Children now are more smarter than the previous generations.

Because of the nice guy that I am, I helped them out again with court paperwork. I produced more evidence to them and the court again. The things I produced to them is for their response to their letter dated February 11, 2000. If I had a law degree, they would be in TROUBLE. Intelligence mean the capacity to learn and to solve problems and difficulties. My help to them.

PETITION/MOTION TO MODIFY CUSTODY

Now comes the time when the Plaintiff, Nelson L. Moody, Sr. request that the Petition/Motion to Modify Custody, filed by the Plaintiff be granted to the fullest extent. Anything that the attorneys request on behalf of their client be denied.. As their focus is not and never have been, "what's in the child's best interest?" according to The Annotated Code of Maryland- Family Law. In support there of states as follows:

1. The defendant denies allegations contained in paragraph 1 (see police report made by defendant).

2. The defendant denies allegations contained in paragraph 2 (see police report made by defendant).

3. The defendant's attorneys states there are no factual assertions (see police report made by defendant).

4. The attorneys state there are no factual assertions (see Brief and Record Extract- Court of Special Appeals of Maryland - September Term 1997 # 479, Petition For Writ of Certiorari- Court of Appeals of Maryland- September Term 1998 # 72, and Petition For Writ of Certiorari- The Supreme Court of The United States- October Term 1998 # 98-6124).

5. The attorneys state there are no factual assertions. The court can either review an administrative appeal according to the "substitution of judgement" standard issue of law arises or it must give difference to the expertise of an administrative agency applying the "rational basis test" standard in question of fact. In the instant case the facts are unquestionable as to what is in the child's best interest and the only determination involves a question of law according to The Annotated Code of Maryland.

6. The attorneys state there are no factual assertions (see Annotated Code of Maryland Family-Law, photos, and knife).

7. The attorneys state there are no factual assertions (tape testimony from child).

8. The attorneys state there are no factual assertions (see Article 1 under The United States Constitution).

9. The attorneys states there are no factual assertions (tape testimony from the child and nightmare the child wrote).

10. The attorneys states there are no factual assertions (see photos of the child).

11. The attorneys states there are no factual assertions (listen to the child's own testimony).

12. The attorneys states there are no factual assertions (listen to the child's own testimony).

13. In paragraph #1 & #2 the defendant, but facts are shown to the attorneys as well as the court system. Paragraph #11 is also denied, everything else the defendant states she admit nor deny as opposed to giving facts, proof, and evidence.

14. I f the defendant denies paragraph #1, then the police report made by her is false. The statements are

contradictory, as well as perjured testimony (as in a court case in The Annotated Code of Maryland).

15. The attorneys knew of the incident on October 3, 1996 as well as November 4, 1996 when The State's Attorney nolle prosequi the case, however they allowed their client to deny paragraph #1 & #2.

16. The defendant mislead The Circuit Court of Maryland in Baltimore City by making the report then denying it in paragraph # 1 & # 2 (as in a court case in The Annotated Code of Maryland).

17. The attorneys knew of and had knowledge of October 3, 1996 and November 4,1996 from the beginning. Their client made the report then deny it ever happening. The attorneys are still presenting false information to The Circuit Court (as in a case in The Annotated Code of Maryland). The Maryland Rules of Professional Conduct were also violated by both attorneys.

18. With the facts, proof, evidence, and pertinent information presented in everything that the Plaintiff (Nelson L. Moody, Sr.) presented to the court system. The attorneys obstructed justice as it pertains to "what's in the child's best interest?". (Art. 26 of The Annotated Code of Maryland, as in a court case in The Annotated Code of Maryland).

19. To this date the attorneys never responded to The Interrogatories dated and stamped January 12, 2000 according to the Md. Rule.

WHEREFORE, the Plaintiff request:

A. Petition/ Motion to Modify Custody be granted to include awarding sole custody of child to Nelson L. Moody, Sr.

B. That the defendant, and the attorneys be ordered to pay the Plaintiff's attorney fees and the cost of these proceedings. The Plaintiff is pro-se.

C. That the Plaintiff be granted such other relief of his cause requires.

D. That the attorneys be punished and be held accountable for their actions.

Very truly yours,

Mr. Nelson L. Moody, Sr.

c. c. Attorney General For The United States
c. c. Attorney Grievance Commission of Maryland

You can see by what's presented to the court and how much is being produced by me, that I mean business. They (knucklehead trainee #1 & #2) don't know who they are dealing with. They better ask somebody.

On Tues. February 12, 2000 my son wasn't sent to my house. On February 16, 2000 my son had problems finding his index cards for a report in school. I told him, "to stay and find them since it pertains to school and his grade". On Fri. February 18, 2000 , while trying to get down my house my son was told by his mother, "she don't drive at night", then left with a girlfriend and never came back. On Tues. February 22, 2000 I got another letter from knucklehead trainee #1. It was the answers to the Interrogatories of which I sent to him on January 12, 2000 in chapter three. It went like this.

Now comes the defendant by her attorney and in answer to the Interrogatories heretofore propounded in this case by the Plaintiff, Nelson L. Moody, Sr. says:

A. The information supplied in these answers to Interrogatories is not based solely upon the knowledge of the executing party, but includes the knowledge of the party's agents, representatives and attorneys, unless privileged.

B. The word usage and sentence structure may be that of the attorney assisting in the preparation of these answers to Interrogatories, and does not necessarily purport to be the precise language of the executing party.

Answer to INTERROGATORY NUMBER 1
Objection, in that Maryland, Courts have held that a party is not required to identify witnesses to be call(a case to support this). Without waiving the objection, the Plaintiff may call Defendant's husband and the child.

Answer to INTERROGATORY NUMBER 2
Objection, see answer #1 without waiving the objection Defendant's husband is a fire fighter, the child is a student.

Answer to INTERROGATORY NUMBER 3
See answer #1.

Answer to INTERROGATORY NUMBER 4
The Defendant is unable to answer this Interrogatory as phrased. (Self explanatory).

Answer to INTERROGATORY NUMBER 5
The Defendant is unable to answer this Interrogatory as phrased (self explanatory).

Answer to INTERROGATORY NUMBER 6
On January 1, 2000 the child made plans with his friends and discussed this with his father. The defendant was not a party to the conversation . On January 5, and 7, 2000 the child arrived home at approximately 6:45p.m. after wrestling practice at school. The defendant advised the child to call the Plaintiff. The Plaintiff apparently told the child not to come over because it was after 6:30p.m..

Answer to INTERROGATORY NUMBER 7
None

Answer to INTERROGATORY NUMBER 8
None.

Answer to INTERROGATORY NUMBER 9
None

Answer to INTERROGATORY NUMBER 10
Objection, an alleged incident occurring in 1996 prior to the previous court order of which the Defendant is allegedly in contempt is not relevant to these proceedings.

Answer to INTERROGATORY NUMBER 11
Objection, see answer 10 without waiving the objection, the Defendant states she did not take the child to any police department on October 5, 1996.

Answer to INTERROGATORY NUMBER 12
Objection, see answer #10

Answer to INTERROGATORY NUMBER 13
Objection, see answer #10

Answer to INTERROGATORY NUMBER 14
Objection, see answer #10 without waiving the objection, no.

Answer to INTERROGATORY NUMBER 15
Each of the courts referred to in the Interrogatory have rejected the Plaintiff's evidence and arguments.

I DO SOLEMNLY DECLARE AND AFFIRM UNDER THE PENALTIES OF PERJURY THAT THE CONTENTS OF THE AFOREGOING ANSWERS TO INTERROGATORIES ARE TRUE AND CORRECT TO THE BEST OF MY

Nelson L. Moody, Sr.

KNOWLEDGE, INFORMATION AND BELIEF.
(these responses were signed by my son's mother).

I got those attorneys so scared they can't even answer questions without beating around the bush. Not to mention defending their clients mess. They better be glad I don't have a law degree. If I had one I would……. On Weds. February 23, 2000 my son's mother had him clean up the basement. As a result of that when asked is she would bring him to my house, he got no response. The attorneys will not get away with nothing they are doing to me. One day I'll have them on the hot seat to see if they can justify their actions. Oh yes, I'll get the right attorney that can see what happened and will represent me against them in a civil law suit. Watch and see.

CHAPTER FIVE -

TEN COUNT

I wanted to keep the heads down on the opposing side by using suppressive letters, laws, and tactics in order to shut them down and up. In the Infantry we call it suppressive fire which is keeping steady fire to keep the enemy down with hope he will surrender. So I added this letter to the suppressive letters, laws, and tactics that went like this : (written on March 1, 2000).

Dear Clerk:

Please except my request to issue summons in reference to my Petition/Motion to Modify Custody currently scheduled for March 29, 2000.

Thank you for your kind cooperation in this matter.

Very truly yours,

Mr. Nelson L. Moody, Sr.
Pro-se

c. c. Top Attorney
c. c. The Defendant

PETITION/MOTION TO MODIFY CUSTODY

Now comes the time when the Plaintiff, Nelson L. Moody, Sr., request that the Circuit Court of Maryland in Baltimore City issue summons for Defendant's husband and the child to testify in court for the following :

1.   Defendant's husband to testify to the fact the child don't get sent to Plaintiff's house like he is suppose to be sent. Also to testify to the fact of the defendant making a police report on October 5, 1996 for an incident which took place on October 3, 1996 of which she (defendant) denies ever happening.

2.   The child (15 years old) to testify that he don't get sent to Plaintiff's house like he is suppose to. Also to testify to the fact that the Defendant made a police report on October 5, 1996 for an incident which took place on October 3, 1996, of which the child was involved.

3.   The officer to testify that the Defendant made the police report on October 5, 1996 for an incident which took place on October 3, 1996 with the complaint # 964J- 2126.

4.   The officer from the crime lab to testify that he took the photos of the child that stem from the police report that the defendant made.

WHEREFORE, the Plaintiff request :

A. That the Defendant and two attorneys, be ordered to pay the Plaintiff's attorney fees and the cost of these proceedings. The Plaintiff is pro-se.

B. That the Plaintiff be granted such other relief and further relief of his cause requires.

C. That the attorneys be punished and held accountable for their actions.

c. c. The Attorney General of The United States
c. c. Attorney Grievance Commission of Maryland
c. c. Commissioner of Baltimore City Police Department

CERTIFICATE OF SERVICE

I HEREBY CERTIFY, that on this first day of March 2000 a copy of this foregoing mail was mailed to:

The Attorney
The Defendant

Mr. Nelson L. Moody, Sr.
Pro-se

On Weds. March 1, 2000 my son wasn't sent to my house on Thurs. March 2,2000. His mother told him, "to call me for why he didn't get sent to my house". Only she can answer her own question, but remember who I'm dealing with. My son was suppose to have came to my house on Fri. March 3, 2000, but didn't. On Sat. March 4, 2000 my son called me at 7:43p.m. to tell me, "he was waiting to be sent to my house". He never showed up.

On Weds. March 8, 2000 he was never sent. From my understanding his mother was gone all day. On Sat. March 11, 2000 my son called me to see if he can stay at his mother's house so he can go to the movies with some friends. I told him, "yes you can". You see I don't mind if he decides to stay for his own reason such as going to the movies with some friends on that end. I don't like it when his mother make excuses to him while messing up my visitation. Men and women out there PLEASE, PLEASE, PLEASE don't be vindictive towards the other parent because the two of you don't get along. That child will make his/her own conclusions of you as they get older. You should hope the child/children are not old enough to where they can see, understand, and put together what's going on. That same child/children who you are playing chess with might have to feed you, choose your nursing home, and plan your funeral. Just a little reminder.

On Weds. March 15, 2000 my son called my house and asked me, "if he can stay at his mother's house to finish his homework on her computer". I told him, "yes" This is his homework and I don't have a computer. On Fri. March 17, 2000 my son's mother was no where to be found to bring him to my house. He ended up coming to my house on Sat. March 18, 2000 at 3:06p.m..

On Weds. March 22, 2000 my son wasn't sent to my house on the account of his mother went to the hair dresser a short time before he was due at my house.

On Weds. March 24,2000 I was in court for my Petition/Motion to Modify Custody. The judge who was before me really didn't want to hear much of what I had to say. She went over some things and knucklehead trainee #2 was up to his old tricks again trying to down play my intelligence. He and this judge was also looking for the Show Cause Order. Once again I came to their rescue and showed the order. The judge gave me that look like "I didn't ask your smart ass self nothing, this is my court room". I laughed on the inside at these attorneys. When it was said and done this judge threaten me by saying, "don't file nothing else in reference to this case or I will dismiss it". I told her, "I'll appeal it because it's my right". She soon told me of my next court date and we were out of there. Again I smiled at knucklehead trainee #2. He just don't know how to take me or what's my next move. Somebody should have told him about me, cause if he didn't know he should have asked somebody.

My son wasn't sent to my house on Sat. March 25, 2000 or Weds. March 29, 2000. The day we went back to court on Fri. March 31, 2000 my son's mother kept him out of school to go to New York to buy some clothes and he never made it to my house. He got back around 10:00p.m.. That's just about how March 2000 ended.

CHAPTER SIX -

MY INJUSTICE

This chapter will be self explanatory and will break down the injustice I got while going through the court system. If you haven't read nothing from "When A Judge Can't Judge (my nightmare of the court system in Baltimore, Md)" and the other chapters in this book you got lost some where along the way. This chapter will certainly give you a complete picture of what I went through.

On April 4, 2000 I wanted the Chief Judge of Maryland know how I really was treated, how I feel about the judicial system in Maryland, and how I don't have any confidence what so ever in the judicial system. I especially don't have any confidence in the judicial system when it comes down to cases like mine when they are open and shut. He or no one else will ever know how this injustice affected me emotionally, mentally, psychologically, physically, and financially.

I was affected in these areas some more than others which I'll always remember. One part of me the court system couldn't touch which was my spirituality and my faith in God . I know this. Thank you Lord for all you have done for and to me. The best in me is yet to come. It was meant for me to go through and endure my situation to help out a great number of men, women, and children. This has made me a much stronger person in a lot of parts in my life.

I wrote this letter to The Chief Judge of Maryland on April 4, 2000:

Dear Judge

I have suffered much injustice while going through the court system in Maryland the way I went through it. The following show just how much injustice I went through. The mental , emotional, and the psychological pain I've suffered can never be replaced.

Injustice is what I got when my son's mother and two of her girlfriends made allegations about me to be someone who I'm not and the Master believed what was said about me with nothing to prove what was said about me.

Injustice is what I got when the Master didn't listen to the doctor and the teacher as they testified on my behalf (as in a case in The Annotated Code of Maryland). The doctor and the teacher are expert witnesses.

Injustice is what I got when my son's mother reported to the police department that her boyfriend (now husband) assaulted our son, and had pictures taken of the injuries which son sustained. She then got to court, recanted her story, and the case got nolle prosequi by The State's Attorney (as in a case in The Annotated Code of Maryland).

Injustice is what I got when Child Protective Services indicated the incident abuse, but failed to intervene by law to petition the court to remove the child from the house of the mother (as in a case in The Annotated Code of Maryland).

Injustice is what I got when a Judge (December 4, 1996) heard my son testify as to where he wanted to live and showed him a nightmare he wrote about his mother and her boyfriend (now husband) were trying to kill him. This was not taken into any kind of consideration of a psychological effect this had on my son (as in a case in The Annotated Code of Maryland), which resulted in actions detrimental to the child (as in a case in The Annotated Code of Maryland).

Injustice is what I got when The Court of Special Appeals of Maryland dismissed my Brief and Record Extract, The Court of Appeals of Maryland denied my Writ of Certiorari, and The Supreme Court of The United States denied my Writ of Certiorari. I've shown all levels of The Judicial System "what's best for the child".

Injustice is what I got when a judge didn't want to hear anything I had to say (January 3, 2000). Another judge dismissed my Petition to Modify Custody (to include changing it) on March 24, 2000.Another judge refused to let my son testify in court on March 29, 2000, along with dismissing my Petition/Contempt of Court I filed on the mother for not sending my son to me like he is suppose to be sent. With no justifiable reason which violated my son's right to testify in court (as in a court case in The Annotated Code of Maryland), also Art. 1 under United States

Constitution- Freedom of speech. She along with the attorney could not find The Show Cause Order that was signed by another judge on January 24, 2000. I showed this to both of them. There was never a written response in the time frame.

Injustice is what I got when the mother and her two girlfriends presented perjured testimony. The mother made a lot of contradictory statements time after time. The attorneys for the mother also presented perjured testimony and paper work to the court time after time and no one picked up on it who should have. As it is outlined in The Annotated Code Of Maryland - what shall be deemed perjury, indictment, contradictory statements, subornation of perjury, and penalty. I listed some cases of people vs. the state and The Attorney Grievance Commission, as well as professional conduct by an attorney from The Rules of Maryland, as well as obstructing justice from The Annotated Code of Maryland.

Still no one is focused on "what's best for the child", but me (as in a case in The Annotated Code of Maryland). After I presented facts, proof, evidence, pertinent information, and creditable witnesses. The court system has allowed these people to damage and ruin my character and reputation along with distorting my life since July 1, 1996. These people to and include the attorneys need to be held accountable for their actions.

With these things in mind the court system in Baltimore Maryland has failed my son as well as myself completely. I have no confidence in the court system when it comes down to justice in a case like mine. By now, of the things I went through I'm sure my son feel the same way also. This same thing can happen to him and his sons.

Since July 1,1996 I have shown "what's in my son's best interest", however it seem like no judge can understand what I've presented to the court as it pertains to my case. Everything that I've presented to the court is self- explanatory. I did represent myself to The Supreme Court, of which some people and some attorneys have said, "the judges don't like it when you represent your self and know the law just as well as they do". Truth is truth and justice is justice no matter who present it to you.

A judge, while judging cases have people's lives in front of them. They can send an innocent man to jail and let a guilty man go based on some one's testimony. It happens a lot. In my case my son will be affected for the rest of his life, because of the judges not judging my case by law, by the book (Annotated Code of Maryland).

Even after Child Protective Services, the hospital, and the police department all have reports of the assault. The police department did an excellent job in this whole case of making the report the mother testified to in reference to the child (complaint # 964J-2126). I congratulate the police department for being the only agency to do their job.

In a section of a newspaper dated March 19, 2000, you experienced a situation of a "sit in protest demonstration" at a Baltimore restaurant which refused to serve colored people were convicted for violating the Maryland criminal trespass law. That protest demonstrated by you and those other 11 students displayed what you believed in and what you were willing to stand for. Because of this protest of civil rights colored people (Negro , African- American) can eat where ever they want to, after being rejected by The Court of Appeals and The Supreme Court. The Court of Appeals considered the case again and overturned the convictions. The overturned convictions was a result of you and the 11 students standing up for what you believed in. That's why I took my case to The Supreme Court.

In closing, if I didn't think nothing was done wrong in my case I would not have taken the time to learn how to represent myself by writing my Brief and Record Extract- September Term 1997 #479, Court of Special Appeals of Maryland, Writ of Certiorari for The Court of Appeals of Maryland- September Term 1998 # 72, Writ of Certiorari for The Supreme Court of The United States- October Term 1998 #98-6124, Letter of Reconsideration For Modification, and Rehearing Letter to The Supreme Court of The United States.

Sincerely,

Mr. Nelson L. Moody, Sr.

   c. c. Attorney General of The United States
   c. c. Chief Justice of The Supreme Court of The
      United States
   c. c. Bar Association
   c. c. Attorney Grievance Commission of Maryland
   c. c. Top Attorney

I just wanted The Chief Judge of Maryland know how I felt about the court system in Baltimore, Maryland. He made a stand for something that he felt strongly about which affected him. He should know how I feel about how I was treated. As the old saying goes, "ignorance is no excuse to the law".

My son wasn't sent to me on Weds. April 5, 2000. On Sat. April 8, 2000 my son stayed at his mother's house on the account of me being out of town on some business. He was never sent on Weds. April 12, 2000.On Thurs. April 13, 2000 I was in court again. I got on the witness stand to tell who I was and why do I feel a change in custody was needed and to talk about the Contempt of Court Order filed by me. I got calenders for the years 1994, 1995, 1996, 1997, 1998, 1999, 2000 and spread them like a deck of cards. I focused on January, February, March, and April of 2000 of my son not being sent to me. You should have seen how stupid the judge looked. The most used phrase of the day was, "my son not being sent to me like he is supposed to be sent". The judge asked me, "What do I mean by the word SENT 4- 5 times". The word sent is self-explanatory. She acted like she didn't understand the word sent.

After I testified my son's mother testified.. While talking to the judge after knucklehead testified I told the judge my son could give his own testimony. She looked at me and mentioned, "she's not letting him testify". I told her, "you are violating his U. S. Constitutional Right of his Freedom of Speech". She then looked at my son slowly and still would not let him testify. I packed up my calenders and both brief cases. I showed her, knucklehead trainee #2, and knucklehead a copy of my book and said to her, "this book is a result of how I was treated in this court system". The three of them really looked dumb founded. An attorney who was behind me also checked out the book.

On day I'm going to get an attorney to represent me in a civil law suit, unless one find me first. I need one who will be able to see by law, without question I was treated very unfair in the court system from the beginning of my case. This attorney will have the courage to challenge the court system as well as making a change for the better of the fathers who are actively involved in the lives of their children and not worry about getting blackballed. I've went to 14 attorneys in Baltimore, Md. Three of them said, "I have a good law suit". I told them, "if I have a good law suit represent me. My book is out, you'll be doing the law suit will work hand in hand and every man who has the same experience I had will come to you". Before we left the court room the judge was suppose to be making another visitation schedule because of my son now being 15 years old now. I'll tell you what happen to this visitation schedule at the end of this book.

On Fri. April 14, 2000 my son wasn't sent to my house like he was suppose to be sent. He came on Weds. April 19,2000 and wasn't sent no more for the month of April. The excuse his mother gave for not sending my son was, none. She went to my son's brother's prom and just never sent him. I was still fed up with what was going on. We (the world) were also watching a custody dispute (international). I wrote The Attorney General of The United States. I have been following this case close from the beginning to the end. I cried every now and then because I could relate to the case in a whole lot of ways. I wrote a letter to The Attorney General of The United States on April 30, 2000:

Dear Ms. Attorney General

As the world watched the international custody battle, the United States Department of Justice stepped in to play referee of this custody battle. I could relate to what was being shown was best. As I kept up with the events that surrounded the case from the beginning, to the number of actions and delays of orders, then finally resulting in force. I wish The Administrative Judge of Baltimore City, The Chief Judge of Maryland, or your self would have investigated and intervene in my custody case the same way as this case.

I represented myself from The Circuit Court of Maryland in Baltimore City to The Supreme Court of The United States in reference to seeking custody of my son. I had facts, proof, evidence, creatable witnesses, and pertinent information. Information that would show any court in this world "what's best for my son"(according to The Annotated Code of Maryland- Family Law, as in cases in The Annotated Code of Maryland). With the question being, "what's in the best interest of the child?". The judges who looked at my case from my understanding are all family judges. I find that hard to believe.

After a wrong conclusion of me by a Master (with nothing to prove what was said about me), my son was assaulted by his mother's boyfriend (now husband). My son carried a knife to school for about three months and also to protect himself until he was caught by school police. The principal knew so did his mother. No report was made, just the knife taken. I t was indicated child abuse by the police department, Child Protective Services, and the hospital I took him to. This showed a change in custody (as in a case in The Annotated Code of Maryland) of which he was involved in domestic violence (certain definitions and cases as it pertains to my case). My son was both the child and the victim. The court system in Baltimore Maryland did nothing to protect him according to the laws of Maryland. The same judicial system that would not investigate allegations of me, that a Master made a conclusion of me with nothing to prove that I was the person I was alleged to be, was the same judicial system that intervened in a international custody case.

In closing, no man who is productively involved in his child/children life should ever go through what I went through in the judicial system. Why would this man (Nelson L. Moody, Sr.) do what he did (learn how to represent himself), to The Supreme Court of The United States if he didn't think nothing was done wrong in his case from July 1, 1996? This is a question no one who I've written to in the state of Maryland and the judicial system can answer. I'm asking and making a request that you step in and intervene in my case.

Sincerely,

Mr. Nelson L. Moody, Sr.

c. c. Chief Justice of The United States
c. c. Chief Judge of Maryland
c. c. Bar Association
c. c. Attorney Grievance Commission of Maryland
c. c. Top Attorney
c. c. The Media

The month of May went by pretty fast to the point where I didn't know it came. The visitation was about the same, however I was through with the court system until someone recognize my problem and bring all of the people who ruined and destroyed my life back to court. It will happen.

Meanwhile knucklehead trainee #1 mailed a letter to The Circuit Court and to me. He wanted the court to order me to pay for knucklehead's attorney fees. I did laugh at the letter and responded with this letter which was written on June 11, 2000.

Dear Top Attorney

You will not threaten me with your letter the way you are doing in reference to something that is unjustifiable as paying the attorney fees for your client.

Your client (with three other names used). These are all names she has used in one way or another since you started to represent her in 1995. Your client works for The City of Baltimore (school system), receives money from Social Security, and might be still receiving money from The Department of Social Services. Ido know the name of her last known case worker. This is well enough for your client to pay her own legal fees just like I paid mine and spent money. This seem to be the only issue you and your partner seem to be concerned about.

I'm glad they're attorneys out there who is not like you and your partner

In closing, I will continue to show and expose your law firm to the media for what it has done to me, ruining my life, destroying my character, slandering my name in court, and the humiliation I have suffered. Someone will pick up on the perjury. What shall be deemed perjury, Indictment, Contradictory Statements, Subornation of Perjury, and Penalty. As well as The Rules of Maryland- Professional Conduct : Intimidating or corrupting jurors, etc. obstructing justice. All of which is found in The Annotated Code of Maryland. A lot of these actions were displayed by your law firm. So you do what ever you feel is necessary, just don't make anymore legal mistakes.

Sincerely,

Mr. Nelson L. Moody, Sr.

c. c. Attorney General of The United States
c. c. Director of Social Services- Baltimore City
c. c. Social Security Administration
c. c. City of Baltimore- Personnel

I'll tell you what response I got from this letter at the end of this book.

CHAPTER SEVEN-

A FATHER'S LOVE (I love you son)

The court system here in Baltimore, Maryland will put an emotional, disturb, abused, etc. child back into the same atmosphere of which he/she was taken from. I f there is a father in the child's life the court system will do a lot to keep the child from being in his/her father's custody. This way the system can always be in control. No judge or court system SHOULD EVER BE INVOLVED IN YOU RAISING YOUR CHILD/CHILDREN. That's first and foremost. God has it father and mother do the raising your children, not someone who don't know you or your child/children.

Before a child is placed with his/her father because of a unfit mother, they(court system and the mother) will want to put the child/children with an aunt, or grandmother before a father who wants his child/children. Wake up court system there are PLENTY OF MEN JUST LIKE ME WHO ARE IN THE LIVES OF THEIR CHILD/CHILDREN. WE ARE HERE TO STAY. TO TAKE IT DEEPER (AFRICAN-AMERICAN, BLACK, NEGRO MEN) SINCE WE ARE THE ONE'S WHO SOCIETY FAILS TO GIVE CREDIT TO. WE ARE JUST AS GOOD AS ANY OTHER RACE OF MEN, HOWEVER ALL MEN ARE AFFECTED, myth. Truth, we are and we are not leaving no time soon.

Men are loving, caring parents too. We have here in The United States so many good fathers (who earn the title "daddy" by way of what he does for his child/children and not because of a sperm cell getting inside of a egg cell) who go through the same situation as mine except no one will investigate by law. With a court system that seem to favor female over male when it comes down to a child/children. No one has any advantage over the other when a child is born.

I have not seen a book that says, "one gender is better at parenting than the other". The focus should be on "what's in the child's best interest?".

As I look around a father can have everything needed (not wanted) for the child/children based on facts, proof, evidence, pertinent information, and creditable witnesses and still it's not good enough for the court system. First of all a court system and no judge should tell you how to raise your child/children, but because in our society we have breakups of fathers and mothers who may have disagreements, some type of legal technicality steps in. You will get my meaning of father, mother, daddy, mommy, as well as parent at the end of this chapter.

When a child/children have a absent father by way of him neglecting his parental responsibilities as the father the child/children suffers deeply. Then the stereotype kicks in that men just can't be fathers (parents) no matter how hard or little they try. To take it deeper (African- American, Negro, Black men) of which society always seem to high light the negative things about us. We are just as comparable as our counterparts when it comes down to "fatherhood".

When a child/children do some things in life as society put it (sex, drugs, crime, pregnancy, drop out of school, etc.) Some times go to the impact the father didn't have on the child/children's life. At that same time a child/children can want to be with his/her father for some time, love, discipline, morals, etc., and for no justifiable reason at all the mother make it her business to intervene with the child/children relationship. If you are a mother doing this and the child can recognize it watch out that child might have to feed you, choose your nursing home, and plan your funeral. Help me out ladies. The ones who keep a child/children from their father. God does the judging and hold you accountable for your actions.

A father can be a great impact on his child/children lives if the mother don't play chess with the child/children. When a father is into his son's life so deep you could bury a house in the dirt. That's good because that's one more good man who is going to be responsible to his child/children as the father plant a seed at an early age, water it, with air and sunshine, then watch it grow. That same boy will carry himself in a way he won't be stereotyped of nothing that is negative in society. That same boy will be groomed like a fresh hair cut when the father is there and the mother don't intervene. He will know how to be a responsible male in every way you can think of if the mother don't……….. That boy would want to emulate his father.

A father can be a great impact on his daughter if the mother don't intervene and get jealous of their relationship. When a father is impacting his daughter's life she would want her husband almost like her father (I say almost because there is nothing like a father's love). A love that's unconditional to his children. Planting that same seed as he planted in his son a father could water, nurture, and watch his little girl grow into a respectful young lady all because of what he put in her. He teaches, shows, guides her etc. to the point where he can stand back and look on his little young lady. Not being ashamed of her for what she does, who she is, and see all because he wasn't there. Mothers if your daughter and her father have a strong secure relationship don't be jealous, but admire and respect it just because she has her father in her life. The daughter will be well respected if the mother............That girl would want her husband to have similar qualities as her father.

If you as a mother didn't have your father in your life for whatever reason that was negative and you watched your mother do some things that you may do to your child/children, remember you only hurt the child/children.

My simple meaning of parent, father, and mother. A parent should be able to raise a boy or girl to be a productive adult. A parent can be a father, a mother, an uncle, an aunt, a grand father, a grandmother, a God father, a Godmother, or a cousin. What ever the case a parent has the job of raising a child/children to reach his/her full potential in life to be a productive person in society, so they can do the same thing for their child/children. A father should be able to raise a boy. A mother should be able to raise a girl.

A father is a person who makes a baby who earn the title "daddy".

A mother is a person who carries a baby who earn the title "mommy".

A title is a name that distinguish someone's character.

Phrases of daddy and mommy which defines the "title". Any man can be a father, but it takes someone special to be a daddy. Because you wear a skirt and bare a child don't make you no mommy.

You can read how I went through a lot with the custody issue question of my divorce as the question "what's in the child's best interest"? Couldn't be answered by the court system. My first book "When A Judge Can't Judge (my nightmare of the court system in Baltimore, Md.)" tells how I was treated. When a man is in his child/children lives in every way you can think of, you as the mother should not play chess, try to break up the bond, mess with, or try to destroy their relationship by playing games. When a man is taking care of his child/children you let him..

This chapter is for fathers, daddy, women, and children who can appreciate and recognize the contents of this chapter.

CHAPTER EIGHT-
WHO JUDGE THE JUDGES?
(God almighty Matt. 7:1,2)

I'm glad that God is sitting high and looking low. For it is him and him alone that will be doing the judging. For it makes me very happy that the judges will have to bow down on their knees and confess Jesus as Lord and Savior. God is the Judge of Judges.

The judges for court dates November 1999, January 2000, March 2000, and April 2000, are all part of The Family Division. Based on what I went through I find that VERY HARD TO BELIEVE. You the reader might find it hard to believe also. As I said before, "I know my case better than the judges before me".

The judges read the case, but didn't understand it what so ever. They heard testimonies, but were not listening to what was being said. Shame on all of them. They (the judges) couldn't handle me representing myself with everything right. Maybe they (the judges) were not trying to acknowledge my intelligence and truth about the whole case. Shame on the judges. In my case it's either right or wrong, truth or lies, justice or injustice, knowledge or no knowledge, knowing or not knowing, "what's best for my son" facts or allegations. There is no in between. What ever the case was throughout my case no one ever had any

JUSTIFIABLE REASONS for what they done with anything (conclusions, dismissed petitions, denied petitions, etc.). I was the only one who could justify any and all things pertaining to my case in court from The Circuit Court of Maryland in Baltimore City to The Supreme Court of The United States.

This have been the first time in my life I have ever been in court for anything. My case went longer than any highly publicized cases that gained national as well as international attention. That's a shame, but I persevered, and endured throughout everything that came my way in the court system.

After going through the court system I was told to attend a class on custody. I laugh, but went for the sake of showing the court system what they were doing was not right. One day someone, somewhere, is going to say, "why the court system put that man Nelson L. Moody, Sr. through all of that unnecessary stuff?". I already have their excuses : we believe what was said by the mother (of which none of the abusive behavior and inappropriate discipline can be proven by no one walking the face of this universe that know my son, his mother, and myself). Second, the Master couldn't justify how and why she came up with a conclusion of me. Third, no one in the judicial system could own up to their NEGLIGENCE and the MISTAKES that they made since July 1, 1996. Shame on them. I 'll stop here, because if my case was judged correctly (judge-the ability to make a decision or form an opinion) then there would not be a need for me to take my case higher than I took it. This is what you do when a judge can't judge. Remember a judge takes an oath to judge cases partially based on facts, proof, evidence, testimony, and pertinent information. The judges before me couldn't do that. I wish they could have given me a reason that would JUSTIFY ANYTHING THEY DID according to The Annotated Code of Maryland, providing their reasons made sense.

To law students and anyone who want to be an attorney PLEASE, PLEASE make sure your client is telling you the truth so the opposing side don't do what I did, because you could be looking STUPID AND INCOMPETENT like the attorneys who went against me. Also you may look like you don't know your profession like the judges who were before me. I knew and still know my case better than the judges, attorneys, and the court system along with a lot more laws as it pertains to my case.

I went through 12 judges from 1995 to 2000 and not one of them could pick up on nothing. The book "When A Judge Can't Judge (my nightmare of the court system in Baltimore, Md.)" and this book "When A Judge Can't Judge Part 2 (the conclusion) tells my whole case in it's entirety. It made me wonder a lot of times if any judge took the time to actually read my case, understand it and able to recognize my paper work was always on the money with every "t" crossed and every "i" dotted.

My case was taken to The Supreme Court of The United States because of truth and principal. You can't compromise or sugar coat the truth. It will come out in time trust me on this one. The principal of showing "what's best for my son" was the most important issue of an ordinance. The right and wrong decisions that were made. The wrong ones by the court system, the judges, and the attorneys. The right decisions were made by me with all the facts, proof, evidence, creditable witnesses, and pertinent information as it is outlined in The Annotated Code of Maryland. ALL I WANTED WAS JUSTICE, instead I got INJUSTICE.

Time will come when society totally except the fact that men are parents too. There is not one book I've seen or read that says, "the female gender is better at raising a child/children than the male gender or vice-versa. Men are and have been reforming their families to the point where the father has a unique and special impact on his child/children. Men can and have the parental responsibilities to teach, lead, love, guide, support, nurture, and discipline their child/children in every way imaginable. Just as the father can talk with his son about life, sex, manhood, duties & responsibilities of a man and a husband. He can also talk with his daughter about life, sex, men, menstrual cycles, etc. and feel comfortable about it. I talk about these issues to my son, daughter, and God daughters and feel comfortable about it. Fathers have the ability to take their child/children to a higher level of life from a father's point of view.

Fathers can also reform his child/children's life when they are torn down, and need a father's love. Fathers offer so much to a child's life to the point where strong bonds start, develop, and become endless.

The court system need to be reformed so cases like mine don't happen again. It will take lots of energy to make it happen. I, myself am going to do my part so my son don't go through what I went through. Also for those men who are in the life of their child/children. This can even help men who are not in the life of their child/children get involved and stay involved. Help me out ladies and children. That child/children of yours may have to feed you, choose your nursing home, and plan your funeral. So be careful.

I, Nelson L. Moody, Sr. believe that a combination of traditional court practices were the reasons used to deny sole custody of child to me. In the past, children were placed with their mothers because the courts felt they were better suited to raise children. While in today's society men are being stereotyped. They are known to not care about or be concerned with the best interest of their child/children. Times have changed where courts need to start relying on evidence, and pertinent information to determine the most suitable home for a child, in which a child should reside.

What a testimony to testify to. I sure hope they (court system, judges, attorneys, son's mother, and her two girlfriends) can give a JUSTIFIABLE REASON for their actions when judgement day comes and they're in front of God Almighty, for he is the judge of judges. This is the answer for the chapter title. Thank you Jesus for being there for me.

CHAPTER NINE -

MY VISION

I have a vision that one day this society in which we live in will come to a complete understanding with full acknowledgment of the truth that men are parents also. I have that vision.

I have a vision that one day parenthood will no longer be looked at as a gender thing (male or female), but a commitment of responsibility to the offspring of two people. I have that vision. I have a vision that one day the responsibility of raising a child/children will not always be favored to the female gender, but to the male gender as well. I have that vision.

I have a vision that one day the male gender will be looked at as a good parent to his child/children to the greatest degree. I have that vision. I have a vision that one day no court system, or judge will have the opinion to tell the male gender when , when not, how, and how long he can see his child/children . I have that vision. I have a vision that one day if a man is in court for his child/children with all the facts, proof, evidence, creditable witnesses, and pertinent information to show "what's best for his child/children", a judge won't hesitate to grant him custody. I have that vision. I have a vision that one day judges will be able to recognize truth and facts as it pertains to a case like mine to protect the child/children and not his/her career. I have that vision. I have a vision that one day court systems in The United States will look at facts, proof, evidence, and pertinent information, while listening to creditable witnesses, before a decision is made with respect to "what's in a child's best interest?". I have that vision.

I have a vision that one day when a woman make a report of domestic violence to the police department, that report stands by itself. I have that vision. I have a vision that one day The State's Attorney will no longer have power of having a domestic violence case nolle prosequi, especially when a child/children are involved. I have that vision. I have a vision that one day a woman will not be able to recant her story in court when a child/children are involved in a domestic violence case, and the child/children are injured. I have that vision.

I have a vision that one day if The State's Attorney nolle prosequi a domestic violence case, especially when a child/children are involved it will automatically be picked up by the next echelon of the judicial system in order to safeguard the child/children. I have that vision. I have a vision that one day Child Protective Services, The Department of Social Services, The School System, and The Court System all cross the same computer system when a police report of domestic violence involving a child/children when reported to the police department. I have that vision. I have a vision that police departments across The United States just keep getting better with cases like mine. I have that vision.

I have a vision that one day court systems will not treat fathers, who are in their child/children live's, like I was treated. I have that vision. I have a vision that one day when a father files for custody of his child/children as he presents facts, proof, evidence, pertinent information, and creditable witnesses, the court system will weigh what's being presented instead of basing judgement, denying the father custody of his child/children because of past traditional court practices. I have that vision. I have a vision that one day when that same man have the medical and educational systems supporting, testifying, and backing him up to show what's best for his child/children it will not be a shadow of a doubt from a judge what's best for the child/children. It's not intended to discredit the mother, but to focus what's best for the child/children. I have that vision.

I have a vision that one day a judge will be able to exercise more common sense when trying to understand a child custody case and the delicacy that surrounds it based on facts, proof, evidence, pertinent information, and creditable witnesses AND NOT BE WORRIED ABOUT CHANGING A PREVIOUS JUDGE'S DECISION IN ORDER TO PROTECT THE CHILD/CHILDREN. One who will not worry about if their friend ship will be hurt, or not be playing golf, cards, etc. together again. I have that vision. I have a vision that one day a judge will be willing and able too admit to his/her mistake, wrong conclusion, or conviction of someone. We all make mistakes and none of us are perfect. I have that vision. I have a vision that one day attorneys be criminally responsible for their actions and not get away with NOTHING. I have that vision. I have a vision that one day attorneys face the same criminal prosecution (jail time and fines) like anyone else. I have that vision.

Last, but not least. I HAVE A VISION THAT ONE DAY CUSTODY OF A CHILD/CHILDREN WILL NO LONGER BE LABELED AS A "CUSTODY BATTLE". IT'S LIKE YOU ARE FIGHTING FOR SOMETHING THAT IS ALREADY YOUR'S. IT SHOULD JUST BE LABELED AS "WHAT'S BEST FOR THE CHILD/CHILDREN". THIS WAY THE FOCUS IS ON THE CHILD/CHILDREN. I HAVE THAT VISION.

This vision that I have is a vision as it pertains to cases like mine.

CHAPTER TEN-

GOD (The Beginning and The Ending)

God is the parent of parents, and after him the biological parents (father and mother) are suppose to have the greatest influence on their child/children's life. We (parents) have the influence to have our child/children succeed or fail in life if we don't influence them. We also play a big part in them respecting themselves so they will respect others and others will respect them. They may not respect themselves to the point where they don't respect others unless we teach them. Love is a feeling of emotions that we can also teach our children about , so they will know what love is . Love is a verb, which means action.

In my case I've gotten some men who question my case as women did in "When A Judge Can't Judge-My nightmare of the court system in Baltimore, Md. In Chapter Ten- MAN, FATHER, AND DADDY (A man who fathered a child that earned the title daddy). Those men were:

1. Men who had no relationship whatsoever with their child/children.

2. Men who had an opportunity to develop a relationship with their child/children, but didn't.

3. Men who gave up on being a part of their child/children life.

4. The one I'LL NEVER UNDERSTAND. The one's who turned their backs on their own

BIOLOGICAL CHILD/CHILDREN, while taking care of a girlfriend or spouse child/children (there is nothing wrong with taking care of and helping a girlfriend or spouse's child/children, BUT PLEASE MAKE SURE YOU TAKE CARE OF YOUR OWN BIOLOGICAL CHILD/CHILDREN FIRST.....). I am 1000% convinced that after a break up all a woman want a father to do is KEEP THE RELATIONSHIP WITH HIS CHILD/CHILDREN. If you are a man out there with a child/children and you are not a part of their life, I'M ASKING YOU TO PLEASE, PLEASE BEGIN TO BE A PART OF YOUR CHILD/CHILDREN LIFE. It is painful growing up without a father in your life. I know this from first hand experience, that's why I'm involved in my children's lives . Please get involved and stay involved for it's never too late on earth. It will be too late if you pass away and God is in front of you judging your involvement with your child/children.

There was never a time where I was challenged by anyone (judges or attorneys) about anything and they were right. That's because they couldn't. This whole case was based on money gained from me to pay my son's mother as opposed to "what's in the child's best interest?". NO MONEY COULD EVER EQUATE THE LOVE OF A CHILD, NONE. The first father didn't do his job, so since I was the one with the long work history it was like I was the one to pay for what he didn't do. The biggest issue they ever had was money not "what's in the child's best interest?". It's a shame my son had to go through this, but at least he was able to see who told the truth and backed it up vs.

who didn't. I'm sure glad he was old enough to see it for himself. His mother showed him the BEST EXAMPLE of how a female can be vindictive towards a man who is involved in his child/children lives by playing chess. I gave my meaning for a female and a woman. In case you forgot, a woman WOULD NOT PLAY GAMES WITH A MAN WHO IS TAKING CARE OF HIS CHILD/CHILDREN. A female on the other hand for no reason whatsoever would.

I went this far (The Supreme Court of The United States), because I had attorneys tell me, "it can't be done, and won't be done without an attorney". I say to those attorneys, "come and get some lessons form me in law on how it's done". You do know who you are. My children know that's not a phrase I allow them to say. I do know anything can be done if you put your mind to it. Besides, with GOD ALL THINGS ARE POSSIBLE. One thing for sure God has my back all the way.

I went the distance, to the end of the road, and still no one (judges or attorneys) could justify NOTHING THEY DID TO THIS DAY. Nor could they give an account for any of their actions. It's all good because one day we all WILL FACE JUDGEMENT by the judge of judges Matt. 7:1, 2.

It's the principal in a case like mine that I had to take it to The Supreme Court of The United States to determine "what's in my son's best interest?" of which did not require no serious thinking, or much thought. Common sense in addition to the law was all that was needed. It was simple to the point a nine or ten year old child could have listened to it and gave a common sense answer.

One thing is for sure you can't compromise, sugar coat, hide, or negotiate the truth. It will come out eventually. To my children I know I told all of you, "there is no such thing as I can't". This will be the only exception to the rule of what I've said. I'll break one of my own laws to say, "you can't compromise, sugar coat, hide, or negotiate the truth". I know you'll understand that's why I love you all.

Just for thought, intelligence over rules ignorance, truth out shine lies, reasons are justifiable, and remember this excuses are unjustifiable. So many doors were closed in my face, and a few were opened at that time. I'm here to tell you God has opened plenty of doors for me that no man can close. The few that are still closed, he is about to open them also.

The court system has really ruined and destroyed my life to a tremendous degree. Some parts I got back, some parts I'll never get back. They couldn't touch my spirituality and my belief in God. I'm glad it's God who will be doing the judging since the judges couldn't judge Matt. 7:1, 2.

You never know when my case may affect your son or sons. Let's change some laws and start enforcing the one's we already have. The attorneys in my case need to be disbarred for practicing law for what I went through and what they couldn't do.

Imagine if I had a law degree. It only takes one person to make a change, especially a positive one. I'm going to commit myself to that change until the court system see it.

God orchestrated my life before I was born and he knew I was going to go through what I went through to help out other men so they can be a part of their child/children lives. The women will appreciate the men more. God will bring you out of it, however it won't be easy. Just keep your faith in God. I've been called a deliverer by two people then I looked up the word. I then went back to Exodus where Moses delivered his people. I've also been called a blessed man, a chosen one, a marked man, a man of courage, a man of integrity, a man of dignity, a man of honesty, man of perseverance, a man of endurance, a man you can trust, a loving father, a man of compassion, a man of strong patience, and a man of tolerance.

I do continue to examine myself to make sure I still fit what was and is said about me. I have also been called a successful man (by my son), a determined man, an admired man, a nice man, a generous man, a thoughtful man, a wise man, an unselfish man, a great man, a loyal man, a respectful man (who gives respect and earns it back). The last ten is how my son out of all people really look at me. I must be doing something right, teaching also. This list could go on by people who KNOW me, and by people who KNOW of me. I'm these things ONLY BECAUSE OF GOD, FOR WITHOUT HIM I'M NOTHING.

It's coming to the day when someone is going to say, "why did Nelson L. Moody, Sr. had to go through and to the extremes of The United States Court System, for custody of his son. After he presented facts, proof, evidence, pertinent information, and creditable witnesses time after time to show what's best for his son?". NO ONE CAN ANSWER THIS SIMPLE QUESTION. It's all good. I've heard judges say, "ignorance is no excuse to the law". I say the same thing to the judges and the attorneys who were before me, "ignorance is no excuse to the law". You know the old saying, "good guys finish last". This good guy, Nelson L. Moody, Sr. will not finish last. It was like everyone wanted to protect their titles and careers, except the police department. They wanted to protect my son.

Some things in life you don't want to do, but have to do. This is one thing I had to do. This time is wasn't cheaper to keep her. It was best to get rid of the stress and the mess.

When a man is before a judge in the future and he proves without a shadow of a doubt "what's best for his child/children, with facts, proof, evidence, pertinent information, and creditable witnesses to his advantage to focus on the child/children. When A Judge Can't Judge (my nightmare of the court system in Baltimore, Md.)-my book of awareness. When A Judge Can't Judge Part Two (the conclusion)-my book of change. These two books are excellent sources of pertinent information. Before a judge makes his/her conclusion, I want him/her to think Nelson L. Moody, Sr. to say, "this guy could be just like him and do what he did". That's the thought I want to leave with judges like the ones I dealt with.

In chapter six I mentioned a judge making a new visitation schedule for my son on April of 2000. I'm still waiting for it. Also the letter I wrote to knucklehead trainee # 1 in reference to him wanting me to pay his client's attorney fees on June 11, 2000, I haven't heard from them and I guess she paid her own attorney fees. Imagine if I had a law degree. You think they look stupid now, just imagine.

The court system then (1996) and now (2001) as I complete writing this book February 20, 2001 @ 1:00 a.m. in the morning, could not justify nothing they done over the course of the above years with facts, proof, evidence, pertinent information, and creditable witnesses. All according to The Annotated Code of Maryland- Family Law.

I was able to infiltrate the court system, learn it's laws as it pertained to my case. I then was able to interpret the laws and used them to my own advantage. Wisdom is the principal thing; therefore get wisdom: and with all thy getting get understanding (Proverbs 4:7). All of this because God is on my side. I can do all things through Christ which strengtheneth me (Philippians 4:13). No one can ever take that away from me.

The cycles and generation curses need to be broken so they can come to an end. Changes need to take place so future generations won't go through what I went through, so I can say my work was not in vain. God has seen my affliction caused by the court system in Baltimore, Md.. He is now ready to deliver me. From him through me I can deliver others in the same situation. While God sits high and looks low, I know he has seen how the judges judged me. I'm so glad he is the judge of judges. God gets the glory, while he allows me to get the victory.

When a Judge Can't Judge - Part Two (The Conclusion)

Nelson L. Moody, Sr.

When a Judge Can't Judge - Part Two (The Conclusion)

Nelson L. Moody, Sr.

When a Judge Can't Judge - Part Two (The Conclusion)

Nelson L. Moody, Sr.

When a Judge Can't Judge - Part Two (The Conclusion)

Nelson L. Moody, Sr.

About the Author

Nelson L. Moody, Sr. born out of wedlock and a product of fatherlessness felt a very deep pain in his heart as a little boy growing up on the Eastside of Baltimore, Md.. The reality of fatherlessness was an early bond that was missed for some unknown reason. A bastard (an illegitimate child). Illegitimate child (against the law; illegal. Born out of wedlock). These were names that were used to describe Nelson L. Moody, Sr.

Nelson L. Moody, Sr. is a man with a vision to change the way society view men as their father hood becomes an issue on whether or not they can effectively perform the task as parents. Men are parents also. A change in the way men think would in fact how society view us, mainly African- American, Black men, Negros. I believe society will rethink the issue of father hood. That vision chapter of mine spell out what I'm focused on.

Nelson L. Moody, Sr. has made it his business to educate men on issues pertained in When A Judge Can't Judge (my nightmare of the court system in Baltimore, Md.) And When A Judge Can't Judge- Part Two (the conclusion) so that women and children will appreciate them better.

Nelson L. Moody, Sr. has NO law schooling that enable him to rise to the Supreme Court of The United States, just common sense. A man who truly loves his children and anyone who knows him know that without a shadow of doubt.

Nelson L. Moody, Sr.
A man, who fathered a child, who
earned the title daddy.

About the Author

A native of Baltimore, Maryland, completing high school in 1981. Obtained various diplomas while serving six years in the military.

Husband, father, Godfather, and uncle who has been involved with children since 1976 as a teenager. A product of not having a father around, but made it his business not to duplicate the same to his children. A man with a passion for encouraging children to do their best in life no matter who tries to put you down. A man who do not believe in the words " I can't and do not allow his children to use them". "With God all things are possible". A man who believes that men can be a great impact on the lives of his child/children if they not only get involved, but stay involved. A man who is determined to change the court system as it pertains to father's rights, as well as changing laws pertaining to father's rights.

www.ingramcontent.com/pod-product-compliance
Lightning Source LLC
Chambersburg PA
CBHW030353290526
45785CB00004B/1721